50 German Appetizer Recipes for Home

By: Kelly Johnson

Table of Contents

- Pretzel Bites with Beer Cheese Dip
- Kartoffelpuffer (German Potato Pancakes) with Applesauce
- Bratwurst Bites with Mustard Dip
- Sauerkraut Balls with Mustard Dipping Sauce
- Bavarian Obatzda (Beer Cheese Spread) with Soft Pretzels
- Currywurst Skewers with Curry Ketchup
- Räucherlachs Canapés (Smoked Salmon Canapés)
- Käsespätzle Bites (German Macaroni and Cheese Bites)
- Bierocks (German Meat and Cabbage Rolls)
- Flammkuchen Bites (German Flatbread with Crème Fraîche and Onions)
- Leberkäse Sliders with Sweet Mustard
- Kartoffelsalat (German Potato Salad) in Crisp Lettuce Cups
- Herring Salad on Rye Bread
- Sauerbraten Meatballs with Red Cabbage Slaw
- Wurstsalat (German Sausage Salad)
- Smoked Trout Mousse on Cucumber Rounds
- German Cheese Fondue with Bread Cubes and Vegetables
- Kohlrabi Schnitzel with Horseradish Cream
- Frikadellen (German Meatballs) with Tangy Tomato Sauce
- Quarkkeulchen (German Potato Pancakes) with Sour Cream and Applesauce
- Rote Grütze Shooters (Red Berry Compote) with Whipped Cream
- Zwiebelkuchen (German Onion Tart) Squares
- Lachsbrötchen (Smoked Salmon Sandwiches) with Cream Cheese and Dill
- Griebenschmalz (Rendered Pork Fat Spread) with Dark Bread
- German Pickle and Cheese Skewers
- Himmel und Erde (Heaven and Earth) Bites with Apples and Potatoes
- Brathering (Marinated Fried Herring) on Pumpernickel
- Stuffed Mushrooms with Bratwurst and Cheese
- Baked Camembert with Cranberry Sauce and Pretzel Crisps
- Matjes Herring Canapés with Pickles and Red Onion
- Käsewürfel (German Cheese Cubes) with Grapes
- Weisswurst Bites with Sweet Mustard and Pretzel Sticks
- Rouladen Skewers with Mustard and Pickles
- Labskaus Crostini (North German Corned Beef Hash) on Baguette Slices

- Obatzda-Stuffed Mini Bell Peppers
- Liptauer Cheese Spread with Radishes and Rye Bread
- Black Forest Ham and Cheese Pinwheels
- Knackwurst Coins with Spicy Mustard Sauce
- Bavarian Ham and Cheese Spread on Pumpernickel Rounds
- German Meat and Cheese Platter with Mustard and Pickles
- Krabbenbrot (North Sea Shrimp Sandwiches) on Rye Bread
- Currywurst Potato Skins with Curry Ketchup
- Gruyère and Leek Tartlets
- Kartoffelbrötchen (German Potato Rolls) with Butter and Sea Salt
- Obatzda-Stuffed Pretzel Bites
- German Ham and Cheese Sliders with Poppy Seed Glaze
- Sauerkraut and Cheese Stuffed Mushrooms
- Sardinenbrot (German Sardine Sandwiches) on Rye Bread
- Würstchen im Schlafrock (Sausages in Blankets) with Mustard Dip
- Pfälzer Saumagen (Palatinate Pork Stomach) Bites with Sauerkraut and Mustard

Pretzel Bites with Beer Cheese Dip

Ingredients:

For the pretzel bites:

- 1 and 1/2 cups warm water (110°F to 115°F)
- 1 packet (2 and 1/4 teaspoons) active dry yeast
- 1 tablespoon granulated sugar
- 4 cups all-purpose flour
- 1 teaspoon salt
- 1/4 cup baking soda
- 1 large egg, beaten
- Coarse sea salt, for sprinkling

For the beer cheese dip:

- 2 tablespoons unsalted butter
- 2 tablespoons all-purpose flour
- 1 cup beer (such as lager or pale ale)
- 2 cups shredded sharp cheddar cheese
- 1/2 cup shredded Swiss cheese
- 1/4 cup cream cheese, softened
- 1/4 teaspoon garlic powder
- Salt and pepper to taste

Instructions:

1. In a large mixing bowl, combine the warm water, active dry yeast, and granulated sugar. Let it sit for about 5 minutes, or until the mixture becomes frothy.
2. Add the flour and salt to the yeast mixture, and stir until a dough forms.
3. Turn the dough out onto a lightly floured surface and knead for about 5 minutes, or until the dough is smooth and elastic.
4. Place the dough in a greased bowl, cover with a clean kitchen towel or plastic wrap, and let it rise in a warm place for about 1 hour, or until doubled in size.

5. Preheat your oven to 425°F (220°C). Line a baking sheet with parchment paper.
6. Punch down the risen dough and divide it into small pieces. Roll each piece into a ball.
7. In a large pot, bring water to a boil and add the baking soda. Drop the pretzel dough balls into the boiling water, a few at a time, and boil for about 30 seconds. Remove them with a slotted spoon and place them on the prepared baking sheet.
8. Brush the tops of the pretzel bites with beaten egg and sprinkle with coarse sea salt.
9. Bake the pretzel bites in the preheated oven for 12-15 minutes, or until golden brown and cooked through.
10. While the pretzel bites are baking, prepare the beer cheese dip. In a saucepan, melt the butter over medium heat. Add the flour and cook, stirring constantly, for about 1 minute to make a roux.
11. Gradually whisk in the beer until smooth. Cook, stirring constantly, until the mixture thickens slightly.
12. Reduce the heat to low and gradually stir in the shredded cheddar cheese, Swiss cheese, and cream cheese until melted and smooth. Stir in the garlic powder and season with salt and pepper to taste.
13. Remove the beer cheese dip from the heat and transfer it to a serving bowl.
14. Serve the warm pretzel bites with the beer cheese dip on the side for dipping.

Enjoy these homemade pretzel bites with beer cheese dip as a delicious appetizer or snack!

Kartoffelpuffer (German Potato Pancakes) with Applesauce

Ingredients:

For the Kartoffelpuffer (German Potato Pancakes):

- 2 lbs potatoes (Russet or Yukon Gold), peeled
- 1 small onion, finely grated
- 2 eggs, lightly beaten
- 3 tablespoons all-purpose flour
- 1 teaspoon salt
- 1/2 teaspoon black pepper
- Vegetable oil, for frying

For the Applesauce:

- 4 large apples (such as Granny Smith or Fuji), peeled, cored, and diced
- 1/4 cup water
- 2 tablespoons lemon juice
- 2 tablespoons granulated sugar (adjust to taste)
- 1/2 teaspoon ground cinnamon (optional)

Instructions:

1. Start by making the applesauce. In a saucepan, combine the diced apples, water, lemon juice, sugar, and cinnamon (if using). Stir to combine.
2. Bring the mixture to a boil over medium-high heat. Once boiling, reduce the heat to low and let it simmer, stirring occasionally, until the apples are soft and cooked through, about 15-20 minutes.
3. Once the apples are cooked, remove the saucepan from the heat. Use a potato masher or fork to mash the apples to your desired consistency. If you prefer a smoother sauce, you can blend it using a blender or food processor.
4. Taste the applesauce and adjust the sweetness and seasoning if necessary. Transfer it to a serving bowl and set aside.

5. To make the Kartoffelpuffer (German Potato Pancakes), grate the peeled potatoes using a box grater or food processor fitted with a grating attachment. Place the grated potatoes in a clean kitchen towel and squeeze out as much liquid as possible.
6. In a large mixing bowl, combine the grated potatoes, finely grated onion, beaten eggs, flour, salt, and black pepper. Stir until well combined.
7. Heat a thin layer of vegetable oil in a large skillet over medium-high heat. Once the oil is hot, spoon about 1/4 cup of the potato mixture into the skillet for each pancake. Use the back of a spoon to flatten the mixture into pancake shapes.
8. Fry the Kartoffelpuffer in batches, cooking for about 3-4 minutes on each side, or until golden brown and crispy. Use a spatula to flip them halfway through cooking.
9. Once cooked, transfer the Kartoffelpuffer to a plate lined with paper towels to drain any excess oil.
10. Serve the warm Kartoffelpuffer with the homemade applesauce on the side for dipping.

Enjoy these delicious Kartoffelpuffer with homemade applesauce as a comforting and satisfying dish, perfect for breakfast, brunch, or as a snack!

Bratwurst Bites with Mustard Dip

Ingredients:

For the Bratwurst Bites:

- 1 lb bratwurst sausages
- 1 tablespoon olive oil
- Salt and pepper to taste
- Wooden toothpicks or cocktail sticks, for serving

For the Mustard Dip:

- 1/2 cup mayonnaise
- 2 tablespoons Dijon mustard
- 1 tablespoon whole grain mustard
- 1 tablespoon honey
- 1 tablespoon apple cider vinegar
- Salt and pepper to taste

Instructions:

1. Preheat your oven to 400°F (200°C).
2. Slice the bratwurst sausages into bite-sized pieces, about 1-inch thick.
3. In a large skillet, heat the olive oil over medium heat. Add the sliced bratwurst pieces to the skillet and cook, stirring occasionally, until browned on all sides, about 5-7 minutes. Season with salt and pepper to taste.
4. Transfer the cooked bratwurst bites to a baking sheet lined with parchment paper or aluminum foil.
5. Bake the bratwurst bites in the preheated oven for 10-12 minutes, or until cooked through and crispy on the outside.
6. While the bratwurst bites are baking, prepare the mustard dip. In a small bowl, whisk together the mayonnaise, Dijon mustard, whole grain mustard, honey, and apple cider vinegar until smooth and well combined. Season with salt and pepper to taste.

7. Once the bratwurst bites are cooked, remove them from the oven and let them cool slightly.
8. Arrange the bratwurst bites on a serving platter and insert wooden toothpicks or cocktail sticks into each piece for easy serving.
9. Serve the bratwurst bites warm with the mustard dip on the side for dipping.

Enjoy these delicious bratwurst bites with mustard dip as a tasty appetizer that's sure to be a hit with your guests!

Sauerkraut Balls with Mustard Dipping Sauce

Ingredients:

For the sauerkraut balls:

- 2 cups sauerkraut, drained and finely chopped
- 1 cup cooked and crumbled sausage or bacon (optional)
- 1 cup shredded Swiss cheese
- 4 oz cream cheese, softened
- 1/4 cup finely chopped onion
- 1 clove garlic, minced
- 1/4 teaspoon caraway seeds (optional)
- Salt and pepper to taste
- 1 cup breadcrumbs
- 2 eggs, beaten
- Vegetable oil for frying

For the mustard dipping sauce:

- 1/2 cup mayonnaise
- 2 tablespoons Dijon mustard
- 1 tablespoon honey
- 1 tablespoon apple cider vinegar
- Salt and pepper to taste

Instructions:

1. In a large mixing bowl, combine the chopped sauerkraut, cooked and crumbled sausage or bacon (if using), shredded Swiss cheese, softened cream cheese, finely chopped onion, minced garlic, caraway seeds (if using), salt, and pepper. Mix until well combined.
2. Take about a tablespoon of the sauerkraut mixture and roll it into a ball. Repeat with the remaining mixture.

3. Place the breadcrumbs in a shallow dish. Dip each sauerkraut ball into the beaten eggs, then roll it in the breadcrumbs until evenly coated. Place the coated balls on a baking sheet lined with parchment paper.
4. Heat vegetable oil in a deep fryer or large skillet to 350°F (175°C).
5. Fry the sauerkraut balls in batches for about 3-4 minutes, or until golden brown and crispy. Use a slotted spoon to remove them from the oil and transfer them to a plate lined with paper towels to drain excess oil.
6. While the sauerkraut balls are frying, prepare the mustard dipping sauce. In a small bowl, whisk together the mayonnaise, Dijon mustard, honey, apple cider vinegar, salt, and pepper until smooth and well combined.
7. Serve the crispy sauerkraut balls hot with the mustard dipping sauce on the side.

These sauerkraut balls with mustard dipping sauce are sure to be a hit at your next party or gathering. Enjoy the delicious combination of flavors and textures!

Bavarian Obatzda (Beer Cheese Spread) with Soft Pretzels

Ingredients:

For the Bavarian Obatzda:

- 8 oz Camembert cheese, softened
- 4 oz cream cheese, softened
- 2 tablespoons unsalted butter, softened
- 2 tablespoons finely chopped onion
- 1 tablespoon sweet paprika
- 1/2 teaspoon caraway seeds (optional)
- 2 tablespoons beer (such as wheat beer or lager)
- Salt and pepper to taste
- Chopped chives or green onions for garnish (optional)

For the soft pretzels:

- 1 and 1/2 cups warm water (110°F to 115°F)
- 1 tablespoon granulated sugar
- 2 and 1/4 teaspoons active dry yeast (1 packet)
- 4 cups all-purpose flour
- 1 teaspoon salt
- 1/4 cup baking soda
- 1 large egg, beaten
- Coarse sea salt for sprinkling

Instructions:

1. To make the Bavarian Obatzda, in a mixing bowl, combine the softened Camembert cheese, cream cheese, and unsalted butter. Use a fork or electric mixer to beat the mixture until smooth and creamy.
2. Add the finely chopped onion, sweet paprika, caraway seeds (if using), beer, salt, and pepper to the cheese mixture. Stir until well combined.

3. Taste the Obatzda and adjust seasoning if necessary. Cover the bowl and refrigerate for at least 1 hour to allow the flavors to meld together.
4. While the Obatzda is chilling, prepare the soft pretzels. In a large mixing bowl, combine the warm water, granulated sugar, and active dry yeast. Let it sit for about 5 minutes, or until the mixture becomes frothy.
5. Add the all-purpose flour and salt to the yeast mixture. Stir until a dough forms.
6. Turn the dough out onto a lightly floured surface and knead for about 5-7 minutes, or until the dough is smooth and elastic.
7. Place the dough in a greased bowl, cover with a clean kitchen towel or plastic wrap, and let it rise in a warm place for about 1 hour, or until doubled in size.
8. Preheat your oven to 425°F (220°C). Line a baking sheet with parchment paper.
9. Punch down the risen dough and divide it into equal-sized pieces. Roll each piece into a long rope and shape it into a pretzel. Place the shaped pretzels on the prepared baking sheet.
10. In a large pot, bring water to a boil and add the baking soda. Carefully drop each pretzel into the boiling water, one at a time, and boil for about 30 seconds. Remove them with a slotted spoon and place them back on the baking sheet.
11. Brush each pretzel with beaten egg and sprinkle with coarse sea salt.
12. Bake the pretzels in the preheated oven for 12-15 minutes, or until golden brown and cooked through.
13. Remove the pretzels from the oven and let them cool slightly.
14. Serve the Bavarian Obatzda with the warm soft pretzels.

Garnish with chopped chives or green onions if desired. Enjoy this delicious Bavarian Obatzda with soft pretzels as a savory and satisfying appetizer!

Currywurst Skewers with Curry Ketchup

Ingredients:

For the currywurst skewers:

- 1 lb bratwurst or German sausage
- Wooden skewers, soaked in water for at least 30 minutes

For the curry ketchup:

- 1 cup ketchup
- 2 tablespoons curry powder
- 1 tablespoon honey or brown sugar
- 1 tablespoon apple cider vinegar
- Salt and pepper to taste

Instructions:

1. Preheat your grill to medium-high heat.
2. Cut the bratwurst or German sausage into bite-sized pieces, about 1-inch thick.
3. Thread the sausage pieces onto the soaked wooden skewers, leaving a little space between each piece.
4. In a small bowl, whisk together the ketchup, curry powder, honey or brown sugar, apple cider vinegar, salt, and pepper until well combined. Taste and adjust seasoning if necessary.
5. Brush the grill grates with oil to prevent sticking. Place the currywurst skewers on the grill and cook for about 8-10 minutes, turning occasionally, until the sausage is cooked through and lightly charred.
6. During the last few minutes of cooking, brush the curry ketchup onto the skewers, turning them to coat evenly. Allow the sauce to caramelize slightly.
7. Once the currywurst skewers are cooked and glazed with the curry ketchup, remove them from the grill and transfer them to a serving platter.
8. Serve the skewers immediately with extra curry ketchup on the side for dipping.

These currywurst skewers with curry ketchup are sure to be a hit at your next barbecue or party. Enjoy the flavorful and spicy taste of this German-inspired appetizer!

Räucherlachs Canapés (Smoked Salmon Canapés)

Ingredients:

- Thinly sliced bread or baguette rounds
- Smoked salmon slices
- Cream cheese or crème fraîche
- Fresh dill, chopped
- Lemon zest (optional)
- Capers (optional)
- Black pepper, freshly ground (optional)

Instructions:

1. Start by preparing the bread or baguette rounds. You can use a cookie cutter to cut out shapes or simply slice the bread into small squares or rectangles.
2. Toast the bread rounds lightly in a toaster or under the broiler until they are golden brown and crispy. Let them cool completely.
3. Spread a thin layer of cream cheese or crème fraîche onto each toasted bread round.
4. Place a slice of smoked salmon on top of the cream cheese or crème fraîche.
5. Garnish each smoked salmon canapé with a sprinkle of chopped fresh dill. You can also add a little lemon zest, capers, or freshly ground black pepper for extra flavor if desired.
6. Arrange the Räucherlachs Canapés on a serving platter and serve immediately.

These Smoked Salmon Canapés are not only visually appealing but also bursting with flavor, making them a perfect appetizer for any occasion. Enjoy!

Käsespätzle Bites (German Macaroni and Cheese Bites)

Ingredients:

For the Käsespätzle:

- 2 cups all-purpose flour
- 4 large eggs
- 1/2 cup milk
- 1/2 teaspoon salt
- 1/4 teaspoon ground nutmeg
- 1 cup shredded Emmental cheese (or Swiss cheese)
- 1/2 cup shredded Gruyère cheese (or any other melting cheese)
- Butter or oil for frying

For serving:

- Chopped chives or parsley for garnish (optional)
- Sour cream or applesauce for dipping (optional)

Instructions:

1. In a large mixing bowl, combine the flour, eggs, milk, salt, and nutmeg. Stir until a thick, smooth batter forms. Let the batter rest for about 15-20 minutes.
2. Bring a large pot of salted water to a boil. Once boiling, reduce the heat to a simmer.
3. Using a spaetzle maker, colander with large holes, or a slotted spoon, press the batter through the holes into the simmering water. The spätzle noodles will float to the surface when they're cooked, which should take about 2-3 minutes. Remove them with a slotted spoon and transfer them to a colander to drain.
4. Once all the spätzle noodles are cooked and drained, heat a large skillet over medium heat. Add a little butter or oil to the skillet.
5. Add the cooked spätzle noodles to the skillet and toss them gently to coat with the butter or oil. Cook for a few minutes until they start to turn golden brown.

6. Sprinkle the shredded Emmental and Gruyère cheese over the spätzle noodles in the skillet. Stir gently until the cheese is melted and the noodles are evenly coated.
7. Remove the skillet from the heat and let the mixture cool slightly.
8. Preheat your oven to 375°F (190°C). Line a baking sheet with parchment paper.
9. Using a small spoon or cookie scoop, portion out small mounds of the spätzle and cheese mixture onto the prepared baking sheet, forming bite-sized balls.
10. Bake the Käsespätzle bites in the preheated oven for about 10-12 minutes, or until they are heated through and the cheese is bubbly and golden brown on top.
11. Remove the baking sheet from the oven and let the Käsespätzle bites cool slightly before serving.
12. Garnish the Käsespätzle bites with chopped chives or parsley if desired. Serve them warm with sour cream or applesauce on the side for dipping, if desired.

Enjoy these delicious Käsespätzle bites as a tasty appetizer or snack! They're sure to be a hit at any gathering.

Bierocks (German Meat and Cabbage Rolls)

Ingredients:

For the dough:

- 4 cups all-purpose flour
- 2 tablespoons granulated sugar
- 1 packet (2 and 1/4 teaspoons) active dry yeast
- 1 teaspoon salt
- 1 cup warm milk (110°F to 115°F)
- 1/4 cup unsalted butter, melted
- 2 large eggs, beaten

For the filling:

- 1 lb ground beef or pork
- 1 small head of cabbage, shredded
- 1 onion, finely chopped
- 2 cloves garlic, minced
- 1 teaspoon caraway seeds (optional)
- Salt and pepper to taste

Instructions:

1. Start by preparing the dough. In a large mixing bowl, combine the flour, sugar, yeast, and salt. Stir to combine.
2. Add the warm milk, melted butter, and beaten eggs to the dry ingredients. Mix until a soft dough forms.
3. Turn the dough out onto a lightly floured surface and knead for about 5-7 minutes, or until the dough is smooth and elastic.
4. Place the dough in a greased bowl, cover with a clean kitchen towel or plastic wrap, and let it rise in a warm place for about 1 hour, or until doubled in size.

5. While the dough is rising, prepare the filling. In a skillet, cook the ground beef or pork over medium heat until browned and cooked through. Drain any excess grease.
6. Add the shredded cabbage, chopped onion, minced garlic, and caraway seeds (if using) to the skillet with the cooked meat. Cook, stirring occasionally, until the cabbage is tender, about 8-10 minutes. Season with salt and pepper to taste. Remove from heat and let the filling cool slightly.
7. Preheat your oven to 375°F (190°C). Line a baking sheet with parchment paper.
8. Punch down the risen dough and divide it into equal-sized pieces. Roll each piece into a ball, then flatten it into a circle about 1/4 inch thick.
9. Place a spoonful of the filling in the center of each dough circle. Fold the edges of the dough over the filling and pinch to seal, forming a ball-shaped pastry.
10. Place the filled pastries seam-side down on the prepared baking sheet, leaving some space between each one.
11. Bake the bierocks in the preheated oven for 20-25 minutes, or until golden brown and cooked through.
12. Remove the bierocks from the oven and let them cool slightly before serving.

Enjoy these delicious bierocks warm as a satisfying meal or snack! They're perfect for any occasion and sure to be a hit with your family and friends.

Flammkuchen Bites (German Flatbread with Crème Fraîche and Onions)

Ingredients:

For the dough:

- 1 and 1/2 cups all-purpose flour
- 1/2 teaspoon salt
- 1/2 teaspoon sugar
- 1/2 teaspoon instant yeast
- 2/3 cup warm water
- 1 tablespoon olive oil

For the toppings:

- 1/2 cup crème fraîche or sour cream
- 1 small onion, thinly sliced
- 2 slices of bacon, cooked and crumbled (optional)
- Fresh chives, chopped (for garnish)
- Salt and pepper to taste

Instructions:

1. In a large mixing bowl, combine the flour, salt, sugar, and instant yeast. Stir to combine.
2. Add the warm water and olive oil to the dry ingredients. Mix until a soft dough forms.
3. Turn the dough out onto a lightly floured surface and knead for about 5-7 minutes, or until the dough is smooth and elastic.
4. Place the dough in a greased bowl, cover with a clean kitchen towel or plastic wrap, and let it rise in a warm place for about 1 hour, or until doubled in size.
5. Preheat your oven to 450°F (230°C). Line a baking sheet with parchment paper.
6. Punch down the risen dough and divide it into equal-sized pieces. Roll each piece into a ball, then flatten it into a thin circle or rectangle, about 1/8 inch thick.
7. Place the flattened dough rounds or rectangles on the prepared baking sheet.

8. Spread a thin layer of crème fraîche or sour cream over each dough round or rectangle, leaving a small border around the edges.
9. Top each Flammkuchen bite with thinly sliced onions and crumbled bacon (if using). Season with salt and pepper to taste.
10. Bake the Flammkuchen bites in the preheated oven for 10-12 minutes, or until the edges are golden brown and crispy.
11. Remove the baking sheet from the oven and let the Flammkuchen bites cool slightly.
12. Garnish the Flammkuchen bites with chopped fresh chives before serving.

Enjoy these delicious Flammkuchen bites as a tasty appetizer or snack! They're perfect for parties or gatherings and are sure to impress your guests with their flavorful toppings and crispy crust.

Leberkäse Sliders with Sweet Mustard

Ingredients:

For the Leberkäse sliders:

- 1 lb Leberkäse (German meatloaf), sliced into thick slices
- Slider buns or small dinner rolls, split
- Butter, for toasting the buns
- Lettuce leaves (optional)
- Sliced tomatoes (optional)
- Sliced onions (optional)

For the sweet mustard:

- 1/4 cup Dijon mustard
- 2 tablespoons honey
- 1 tablespoon apple cider vinegar
- Pinch of salt

Instructions:

1. Preheat your grill or a large skillet over medium-high heat.
2. While the grill or skillet is heating up, prepare the sweet mustard. In a small bowl, whisk together the Dijon mustard, honey, apple cider vinegar, and a pinch of salt until well combined. Adjust sweetness and tartness according to your taste preferences. Set aside.
3. If using a grill, lightly oil the grill grates. Grill the Leberkäse slices for 3-4 minutes on each side, or until they are heated through and have grill marks. If using a skillet, heat a little oil in the skillet and cook the Leberkäse slices for about 3-4 minutes on each side, until golden brown and heated through.
4. While the Leberkäse is cooking, spread a thin layer of butter on the split slider buns or dinner rolls. Toast them on the grill or in a skillet until they are lightly golden brown and crispy.

5. To assemble the sliders, place a grilled Leberkäse slice on the bottom half of each bun. Top with lettuce leaves, sliced tomatoes, and sliced onions if desired.
6. Drizzle a generous amount of sweet mustard over the Leberkäse slices.
7. Place the top half of each bun on top of the Leberkäse and press down gently to secure.
8. Serve the Leberkäse sliders immediately, while still warm, with extra sweet mustard on the side for dipping.

These Leberkäse sliders with sweet mustard are sure to be a hit at your next gathering or party. They're flavorful, satisfying, and easy to make! Enjoy!

Kartoffelsalat (German Potato Salad) in Crisp Lettuce Cups

Ingredients:

For the German Potato Salad:

- 2 lbs potatoes (Yukon Gold or red potatoes), peeled and diced
- 1 small onion, finely chopped
- 4 slices bacon, diced
- 1/4 cup apple cider vinegar
- 2 tablespoons vegetable oil or bacon drippings
- 1 tablespoon granulated sugar
- 1 teaspoon Dijon mustard
- Salt and pepper to taste
- Chopped fresh parsley for garnish

For serving:

- Crisp lettuce leaves (such as iceberg or butter lettuce)

Instructions:

1. Place the diced potatoes in a large pot and cover them with water. Bring the water to a boil, then reduce the heat to medium-low and simmer the potatoes for about 10-15 minutes, or until tender but still firm. Drain the potatoes and let them cool slightly.
2. While the potatoes are cooking, heat a skillet over medium heat. Add the diced bacon and cook until crispy. Remove the bacon from the skillet and drain on paper towels. Reserve the bacon drippings in the skillet.
3. In the same skillet with the bacon drippings, add the finely chopped onion. Cook until the onion is softened and translucent, about 3-4 minutes.
4. In a small bowl, whisk together the apple cider vinegar, vegetable oil or bacon drippings, granulated sugar, Dijon mustard, salt, and pepper to make the dressing.
5. Place the cooked and slightly cooled potatoes in a large mixing bowl. Add the cooked onions and crispy bacon.

6. Pour the dressing over the potato mixture and gently toss until well combined and evenly coated. Adjust seasoning to taste with additional salt and pepper if needed.
7. To serve, arrange the crisp lettuce leaves on a platter or individual serving plates.
8. Spoon the German potato salad onto the lettuce leaves, filling each cup generously.
9. Garnish the potato salad cups with chopped fresh parsley for a pop of color and flavor.
10. Serve the Kartoffelsalat in crisp lettuce cups immediately as a refreshing and flavorful appetizer or side dish.

Enjoy this delightful twist on German potato salad, served in crisp lettuce cups, at your next gathering or as a light and satisfying meal!

Herring Salad on Rye Bread

Ingredients:

For the herring salad:

- 1 cup pickled herring fillets, drained and chopped
- 1/2 cup sour cream or crème fraîche
- 2 tablespoons mayonnaise
- 1 tablespoon Dijon mustard
- 1 small onion, finely chopped
- 1 tablespoon capers, drained and chopped (optional)
- Salt and pepper to taste
- Chopped fresh dill or chives for garnish

For serving:

- Rye bread slices or rye bread rolls
- Butter (optional)
- Sliced cucumber, radishes, or other vegetables for garnish (optional)

Instructions:

1. In a mixing bowl, combine the chopped pickled herring fillets, sour cream or crème fraîche, mayonnaise, Dijon mustard, finely chopped onion, and chopped capers (if using). Stir until well combined.
2. Season the herring salad with salt and pepper to taste. Adjust the seasoning if needed.
3. Cover the bowl with plastic wrap and refrigerate the herring salad for at least 30 minutes to allow the flavors to meld together.
4. To serve, spread a thin layer of butter (if desired) on the rye bread slices or rolls.
5. Spoon a generous portion of the chilled herring salad onto each rye bread slice or roll.
6. Garnish the herring salad with chopped fresh dill or chives for a burst of flavor and freshness.

7. Optionally, serve the herring salad sandwiches with sliced cucumber, radishes, or other vegetables on the side for added crunch and freshness.
8. Serve the herring salad on rye bread immediately as an open-faced sandwich or as a light and refreshing appetizer.

Enjoy this delicious and traditional herring salad on rye bread as a flavorful and satisfying dish that's perfect for any occasion!

Sauerbraten Meatballs with Red Cabbage Slaw

Ingredients:

For the Sauerbraten Meatballs:

- 1 lb ground beef
- 1/2 cup breadcrumbs
- 1/4 cup milk
- 1 small onion, finely chopped
- 2 cloves garlic, minced
- 2 tablespoons red wine vinegar
- 2 tablespoons brown sugar
- 2 tablespoons Dijon mustard
- 1 tablespoon Worcestershire sauce
- 1 teaspoon ground ginger
- 1/2 teaspoon ground cloves
- Salt and pepper to taste
- 1 tablespoon vegetable oil, for frying

For the Red Cabbage Slaw:

- 3 cups shredded red cabbage
- 1 large carrot, grated
- 1/4 cup mayonnaise
- 2 tablespoons apple cider vinegar
- 1 tablespoon honey
- Salt and pepper to taste
- Chopped fresh parsley or chives for garnish (optional)

Instructions:

1. In a large mixing bowl, combine the ground beef, breadcrumbs, milk, finely chopped onion, minced garlic, red wine vinegar, brown sugar, Dijon mustard, Worcestershire sauce, ground ginger, ground cloves, salt, and pepper. Mix until well combined.
2. Shape the mixture into meatballs, about 1 inch in diameter.

3. Heat the vegetable oil in a large skillet over medium heat. Add the meatballs to the skillet and cook until browned on all sides and cooked through, about 10-12 minutes. Remove the meatballs from the skillet and set aside.
4. In a separate mixing bowl, combine the shredded red cabbage and grated carrot.
5. In a small bowl, whisk together the mayonnaise, apple cider vinegar, honey, salt, and pepper to make the dressing.
6. Pour the dressing over the red cabbage and carrot mixture and toss until well coated.
7. To serve, arrange the sauerbraten meatballs on a platter or individual serving plates. Serve the red cabbage slaw alongside the meatballs.
8. Garnish the red cabbage slaw with chopped fresh parsley or chives if desired.
9. Serve the sauerbraten meatballs with red cabbage slaw immediately as a delicious and satisfying meal.

Enjoy the tangy flavors of sauerbraten meatballs paired with the crispness of red cabbage slaw for a delightful and comforting dish!

Wurstsalat (German Sausage Salad)

Ingredients:

- 1 lb German-style sausage (such as Fleischwurst, Lyoner, or Bologna), thinly sliced
- 1 small onion, thinly sliced
- 1 tablespoon vegetable oil
- 2 tablespoons white wine vinegar
- 1 tablespoon mustard (preferably sweet or Bavarian mustard)
- 1 tablespoon chopped fresh parsley
- Salt and pepper to taste
- Optional toppings: sliced pickles, diced bell peppers, chopped chives

Instructions:

1. In a large mixing bowl, combine the thinly sliced sausage and onion.
2. In a small bowl, whisk together the vegetable oil, white wine vinegar, and mustard until well combined.
3. Pour the dressing over the sausage and onion mixture. Toss until the sausage and onion are evenly coated.
4. Add the chopped fresh parsley to the salad and toss again to combine.
5. Season the Wurstsalat with salt and pepper to taste. Adjust seasoning if needed.
6. If desired, add optional toppings such as sliced pickles, diced bell peppers, or chopped chives for extra flavor and texture.
7. Cover the bowl with plastic wrap and refrigerate the Wurstsalat for at least 30 minutes to allow the flavors to meld together.
8. Serve the Wurstsalat chilled as an appetizer, light lunch, or side dish. It pairs well with crusty bread or pretzels.

Enjoy the tangy and savory flavors of this traditional German sausage salad! It's a refreshing and satisfying dish that's sure to be a hit with your family and friends.

Smoked Trout Mousse on Cucumber Rounds

Ingredients:

For the smoked trout mousse:

- 8 oz smoked trout fillets, skin removed
- 4 oz cream cheese, softened
- 2 tablespoons sour cream
- 1 tablespoon lemon juice
- 1 tablespoon chopped fresh dill
- Salt and pepper to taste

For serving:

- 2 English cucumbers, sliced into rounds
- Fresh dill sprigs for garnish

Instructions:

1. In a food processor, combine the smoked trout fillets, cream cheese, sour cream, lemon juice, and chopped fresh dill. Pulse until smooth and creamy. If the mixture is too thick, you can add a little more sour cream or lemon juice to reach your desired consistency. Season with salt and pepper to taste.
2. Transfer the smoked trout mousse to a piping bag fitted with a star tip, or simply use a spoon for spreading.
3. Arrange the cucumber rounds on a serving platter.
4. Pipe or spread a small amount of the smoked trout mousse onto each cucumber round.
5. Garnish each cucumber round with a small sprig of fresh dill.
6. Serve the smoked trout mousse on cucumber rounds immediately as a delicious and elegant appetizer.

Enjoy the creamy texture and delicate flavor of the smoked trout mousse paired with the crispness of the cucumber rounds. It's the perfect appetizer for any occasion!

German Cheese Fondue with Bread Cubes and Vegetables

Ingredients:

For the cheese fondue:

- 1 lb Emmental cheese, grated
- 1 lb Gruyère cheese, grated
- 2 tablespoons cornstarch
- 1 clove garlic, halved
- 1 cup dry white wine (such as Riesling or Gewürztraminer)
- 1 tablespoon lemon juice
- 1 tablespoon Kirsch (optional)
- Pinch of nutmeg
- Salt and pepper to taste

For serving:

- Cubed crusty bread (such as French baguette or sourdough)
- Assorted vegetables (such as blanched broccoli florets, cauliflower florets, baby carrots, cherry tomatoes, and sliced bell peppers)

Instructions:

1. In a large mixing bowl, toss the grated Emmental and Gruyère cheeses with the cornstarch until evenly coated.
2. Rub the inside of a fondue pot or heavy-bottomed saucepan with the halved garlic clove.
3. Pour the white wine into the fondue pot and heat it over medium heat until it starts to simmer.
4. Gradually add the grated cheese mixture to the simmering wine, stirring constantly in a figure-eight motion until the cheese is melted and smooth.
5. Stir in the lemon juice, Kirsch (if using), nutmeg, salt, and pepper to taste. Continue to cook for a few more minutes until the fondue is thick and creamy.

6. Adjust the heat to keep the fondue warm and smooth. If the fondue becomes too thick, you can add a little more wine to thin it out.
7. To serve, place the fondue pot on a fondue burner or trivet on the table.
8. Arrange the cubed bread and assorted vegetables on a platter or individual plates.
9. Spear a piece of bread or vegetable with a fondue fork and dip it into the warm cheese fondue, swirling it to coat.
10. Enjoy the German cheese fondue with bread cubes and vegetables, savoring each bite of gooey, melted cheese and crunchy bread or crisp vegetables.
11. Stir the fondue occasionally to prevent it from scorching on the bottom, and add more wine if needed to maintain the desired consistency.
12. Have fun and enjoy the interactive dining experience with your guests!

German cheese fondue is a fun and delicious way to enjoy a cozy meal together. Dip, swirl, and savor the cheesy goodness with your favorite bread cubes and vegetables!

Kohlrabi Schnitzel with Horseradish Cream

Ingredients:

For the kohlrabi schnitzel:

- 2 large kohlrabi bulbs, peeled and thinly sliced into rounds
- 1/2 cup all-purpose flour
- 2 large eggs, beaten
- 1 cup breadcrumbs
- Salt and pepper to taste
- Vegetable oil for frying

For the horseradish cream:

- 1/2 cup sour cream or Greek yogurt
- 2 tablespoons prepared horseradish
- 1 tablespoon lemon juice
- 1 tablespoon chopped fresh parsley (optional)
- Salt and pepper to taste

Instructions:

1. Prepare the kohlrabi schnitzel: Place the thinly sliced kohlrabi rounds between two layers of paper towels and press down gently to remove excess moisture.
2. Set up a breading station with three shallow bowls: one with flour, one with beaten eggs, and one with breadcrumbs seasoned with salt and pepper.
3. Dredge each kohlrabi round in flour, shaking off any excess. Dip it into the beaten eggs, allowing any excess to drip off. Then coat it evenly with breadcrumbs, pressing gently to adhere.
4. Heat vegetable oil in a large skillet over medium-high heat. Carefully add the breaded kohlrabi rounds to the hot oil in batches, making sure not to overcrowd the skillet. Fry until golden brown and crispy on both sides, about 2-3 minutes per side. Transfer to a paper towel-lined plate to drain excess oil.
5. Prepare the horseradish cream: In a small bowl, whisk together the sour cream or Greek yogurt, prepared horseradish, lemon juice, chopped fresh parsley (if using), salt, and pepper until smooth and well combined.

6. Serve the crispy kohlrabi schnitzel hot, accompanied by the tangy horseradish cream sauce for dipping or drizzling.
7. Garnish with additional chopped parsley if desired, and serve immediately as a flavorful and satisfying vegetarian dish.

Enjoy the crispy texture and mild, sweet flavor of the kohlrabi schnitzel, complemented by the zesty kick of the horseradish cream sauce! It's a unique and delicious way to enjoy this versatile vegetable.

Frikadellen (German Meatballs) with Tangy Tomato Sauce

Ingredients:

For the Frikadellen:

- 1 lb ground beef
- 1 small onion, finely chopped
- 1/4 cup breadcrumbs
- 1 egg
- 1 tablespoon mustard
- 1 tablespoon Worcestershire sauce
- 1 teaspoon paprika
- Salt and pepper to taste
- Vegetable oil for frying

For the Tangy Tomato Sauce:

- 1 tablespoon olive oil
- 1 small onion, finely chopped
- 2 cloves garlic, minced
- 1 can (14 oz) diced tomatoes
- 2 tablespoons tomato paste
- 1 tablespoon brown sugar
- 1 tablespoon apple cider vinegar
- 1 teaspoon dried oregano
- Salt and pepper to taste

Instructions:

1. In a large mixing bowl, combine the ground beef, finely chopped onion, breadcrumbs, egg, mustard, Worcestershire sauce, paprika, salt, and pepper. Mix until well combined.
2. Shape the mixture into meatballs, about 1 to 1.5 inches in diameter.

3. Heat vegetable oil in a large skillet over medium heat. Add the meatballs to the skillet in batches, making sure not to overcrowd them. Cook until browned on all sides and cooked through, about 8-10 minutes. Transfer the cooked meatballs to a plate lined with paper towels to drain excess oil.
4. In the same skillet, heat olive oil over medium heat. Add the finely chopped onion and minced garlic, and cook until softened and fragrant, about 2-3 minutes.
5. Stir in the diced tomatoes, tomato paste, brown sugar, apple cider vinegar, dried oregano, salt, and pepper. Bring the sauce to a simmer and cook for 10-15 minutes, stirring occasionally, until the flavors are well blended and the sauce has thickened slightly.
6. Return the cooked meatballs to the skillet, stirring gently to coat them in the tangy tomato sauce. Simmer for an additional 5 minutes to heat the meatballs through.
7. Serve the Frikadellen with tangy tomato sauce hot, garnished with chopped fresh parsley or chives if desired.
8. Enjoy these flavorful German meatballs with a tangy tomato sauce served alongside mashed potatoes, noodles, or crusty bread for a hearty and satisfying meal!

These Frikadellen with tangy tomato sauce are sure to be a hit with your family and friends. They're flavorful, comforting, and perfect for any occasion!

Quarkkeulchen (German Potato Pancakes) with Sour Cream and Applesauce

Ingredients:

For the Quarkkeulchen:

- 2 lbs potatoes, peeled and grated
- 1 small onion, finely chopped
- 2 eggs
- 1/4 cup all-purpose flour
- 1/4 cup quark or Greek yogurt
- 2 tablespoons chopped fresh parsley
- Salt and pepper to taste
- Vegetable oil for frying

For serving:

- Sour cream
- Applesauce
- Additional chopped fresh parsley for garnish (optional)

Instructions:

1. Place the grated potatoes in a clean kitchen towel and squeeze out excess moisture.
2. In a large mixing bowl, combine the grated potatoes, finely chopped onion, eggs, flour, quark or Greek yogurt, chopped fresh parsley, salt, and pepper. Mix until well combined.
3. Heat vegetable oil in a large skillet over medium heat.
4. Drop spoonfuls of the potato mixture into the hot oil, flattening them slightly with the back of the spoon to form pancakes.
5. Fry the Quarkkeulchen in batches until golden brown and crispy on both sides, about 3-4 minutes per side. Use a spatula to flip them halfway through cooking.
6. Transfer the cooked Quarkkeulchen to a plate lined with paper towels to drain excess oil.

7. Serve the Quarkkeulchen hot, accompanied by sour cream and applesauce for dipping or drizzling.
8. Garnish with additional chopped fresh parsley if desired.

Enjoy these delicious German potato pancakes with sour cream and applesauce for a tasty and comforting meal or snack! They're crispy on the outside, soft and fluffy on the inside, and perfect for any time of day.

Rote Grütze Shooters (Red Berry Compote) with Whipped Cream

Ingredients:

For the Rote Grütze:

- 2 cups mixed red berries (such as strawberries, raspberries, and red currants), fresh or frozen
- 1/2 cup granulated sugar
- 1/4 cup water
- 2 tablespoons cornstarch
- 2 tablespoons cold water
- Juice of 1/2 lemon
- 1 teaspoon vanilla extract

For the whipped cream:

- 1 cup heavy cream
- 2 tablespoons powdered sugar
- 1 teaspoon vanilla extract

Instructions:

1. In a medium saucepan, combine the mixed red berries, granulated sugar, 1/4 cup water, lemon juice, and vanilla extract. Bring to a simmer over medium heat, stirring occasionally.
2. In a small bowl, mix the cornstarch with 2 tablespoons of cold water until smooth. Add the cornstarch mixture to the simmering berry mixture, stirring constantly.
3. Cook the berry mixture for an additional 2-3 minutes, or until thickened. Remove from heat and let it cool slightly.
4. Strain the berry compote through a fine mesh sieve to remove any seeds or pulp. Discard the solids and transfer the strained compote to a bowl. Let it cool completely.

5. In a mixing bowl, whip the heavy cream with powdered sugar and vanilla extract until stiff peaks form.
6. To assemble the shooters, spoon a layer of the cooled Rote Grütze into shot glasses or small serving glasses, filling them about halfway.
7. Top each glass with a dollop of whipped cream.
8. Repeat the layers with another spoonful of Rote Grütze and another dollop of whipped cream.
9. Garnish the shooters with additional fresh berries or mint leaves if desired.
10. Serve the Rote Grütze shooters immediately as a refreshing and elegant dessert.

Enjoy the sweet and tangy flavors of the Rote Grütze paired with the creamy richness of the whipped cream in these delightful shooters! They're perfect for parties, gatherings, or any time you're craving a sweet treat.

Zwiebelkuchen (German Onion Tart) Squares

Ingredients:

For the crust:

- 1 and 1/2 cups all-purpose flour
- 1/2 teaspoon salt
- 1/2 cup unsalted butter, cold and cubed
- 1/4 cup ice water

For the filling:

- 4 large onions, thinly sliced
- 4 slices bacon, diced
- 1 tablespoon butter
- 2 eggs
- 1/2 cup sour cream
- 1/2 cup milk
- Salt and pepper to taste
- 1/4 teaspoon ground nutmeg
- Chopped fresh parsley for garnish (optional)

Instructions:

1. Preheat your oven to 375°F (190°C). Grease a 9x13 inch baking dish or line it with parchment paper.
2. To make the crust, in a large mixing bowl, combine the flour and salt. Cut in the cold, cubed butter using a pastry cutter or your fingers until the mixture resembles coarse crumbs.
3. Gradually add the ice water, 1 tablespoon at a time, mixing until the dough comes together and forms a ball. Wrap the dough in plastic wrap and refrigerate for at least 30 minutes.

4. Roll out the chilled dough on a lightly floured surface into a rectangle slightly larger than your baking dish. Transfer the dough to the prepared baking dish, pressing it into the bottom and up the sides.
5. Prick the bottom of the crust with a fork and blind bake it in the preheated oven for 10-12 minutes, until lightly golden brown. Remove from the oven and set aside.
6. While the crust is baking, prepare the filling. In a large skillet, cook the diced bacon until crispy. Remove the bacon from the skillet and drain on paper towels.
7. In the same skillet, add 1 tablespoon of butter and the thinly sliced onions. Cook over medium heat, stirring occasionally, until the onions are caramelized and golden brown, about 15-20 minutes.
8. In a separate bowl, whisk together the eggs, sour cream, milk, salt, pepper, and ground nutmeg until well combined.
9. Spread the caramelized onions evenly over the partially baked crust, then sprinkle the crispy bacon on top.
10. Pour the egg mixture over the onions and bacon in the crust, spreading it out evenly.
11. Return the tart to the oven and bake for an additional 25-30 minutes, or until the filling is set and the top is golden brown.
12. Remove the Zwiebelkuchen from the oven and let it cool slightly before slicing into squares.
13. Garnish with chopped fresh parsley if desired, and serve warm or at room temperature.

Enjoy these savory and flavorful Zwiebelkuchen squares as a delicious appetizer, side dish, or snack! They're perfect for sharing with family and friends.

Lachsbrötchen (Smoked Salmon Sandwiches) with Cream Cheese and Dill

Ingredients:

- 8 slices of your favorite bread (such as rye, whole wheat, or sourdough)
- 8 oz smoked salmon slices
- 4 oz cream cheese, softened
- 2 tablespoons chopped fresh dill
- 1 tablespoon lemon juice
- Salt and pepper to taste
- Thinly sliced cucumber (optional)
- Thinly sliced red onion (optional)
- Capers (optional)

Instructions:

1. In a small mixing bowl, combine the softened cream cheese, chopped fresh dill, lemon juice, salt, and pepper. Mix until well combined.
2. Toast the slices of bread until golden brown and crisp.
3. Spread a generous layer of the dill cream cheese mixture onto each slice of toasted bread.
4. Top each slice of bread with a layer of smoked salmon slices.
5. If desired, add thinly sliced cucumber, red onion, and capers on top of the smoked salmon for extra flavor and texture.
6. Serve the Lachsbrötchen immediately, or cover and refrigerate until ready to serve.
7. Optionally, garnish with additional fresh dill before serving.

Enjoy these delicious Lachsbrötchen sandwiches with cream cheese and dill as a tasty and elegant appetizer or light meal! They're sure to be a hit with your family and friends.

Griebenschmalz (Rendered Pork Fat Spread) with Dark Bread

Ingredients:

- 1 lb pork fat with skin (leaf lard or back fat)
- 1 small onion, finely chopped
- 1 small apple, peeled, cored, and finely chopped
- 1 teaspoon salt
- 1/2 teaspoon ground black pepper
- 1/4 teaspoon ground caraway seeds (optional)
- Dark bread, such as pumpernickel or rye, sliced

Instructions:

1. Cut the pork fat into small cubes and place them in a large, heavy-bottomed pot or Dutch oven.
2. Cook the pork fat over low heat, stirring occasionally, until it has rendered down and turned into liquid fat. This process can take several hours, so be patient.
3. Once the fat has rendered completely and the pork cracklings (Grieben) are crispy and golden brown, remove them from the pot with a slotted spoon and drain them on paper towels. Reserve the cracklings for later.
4. Return the rendered pork fat to the pot and add the finely chopped onion and apple.
5. Cook the onion and apple in the pork fat over low heat, stirring occasionally, until they are soft and golden brown, about 20-30 minutes.
6. Remove the pot from the heat and let the mixture cool slightly.
7. Transfer the cooked onion and apple mixture to a food processor and pulse until smooth. Alternatively, you can use a potato masher or fork to mash the mixture by hand.
8. Season the Griebenschmalz with salt, pepper, and ground caraway seeds (if using), to taste.
9. Transfer the Griebenschmalz to a serving bowl and stir in the reserved crispy pork cracklings.
10. Serve the Griebenschmalz at room temperature with slices of dark bread.

Enjoy this rich and flavorful Griebenschmalz spread on dark bread as a delicious and traditional German treat!

German Pickle and Cheese Skewers

Ingredients:

- 1 block of your favorite cheese (such as cheddar, gouda, or Swiss), cut into cubes
- German-style pickles (such as cornichons or gherkins), whole or sliced
- Cherry tomatoes (optional)
- Wooden skewers or toothpicks

Instructions:

1. If using wooden skewers, soak them in water for about 30 minutes to prevent them from burning.
2. Assemble the skewers by alternating cubes of cheese, whole or sliced German pickles, and cherry tomatoes (if using) onto the skewers or toothpicks.
3. Repeat the process until you've filled all the skewers or used up all the ingredients.
4. Arrange the pickle and cheese skewers on a serving platter.
5. Serve immediately as a tasty appetizer or snack.

These German pickle and cheese skewers are perfect for parties, gatherings, or as a simple and satisfying snack any time of day. Enjoy the combination of flavors and textures in each bite!

Himmel und Erde (Heaven and Earth) Bites with Apples and Potatoes

Ingredients:

- 2 large potatoes, peeled and cubed
- 2 apples, peeled, cored, and cubed
- 4 slices bacon, diced
- 1 onion, finely chopped
- 2 tablespoons butter
- Salt and pepper to taste
- Chopped fresh parsley for garnish (optional)

Instructions:

1. Place the cubed potatoes in a pot of salted water. Bring to a boil and cook until the potatoes are tender, about 10-15 minutes. Drain and set aside.
2. In a large skillet, cook the diced bacon over medium heat until crispy. Remove the bacon from the skillet and drain on paper towels.
3. In the same skillet, add the chopped onion and cook until softened and translucent, about 5 minutes.
4. Add the cubed apples to the skillet with the onions and cook until they are soft but still hold their shape, about 5-7 minutes.
5. In a separate skillet, melt the butter over medium heat. Add the cooked potatoes to the skillet and cook until they are golden brown and crispy on the outside, about 5-7 minutes.
6. Combine the cooked bacon, onions, and apples in the skillet with the potatoes. Stir gently to combine.
7. Season the Himmel und Erde mixture with salt and pepper to taste.
8. Transfer the mixture to a serving dish and garnish with chopped fresh parsley if desired.
9. Serve the Himmel und Erde bites warm as a delicious and comforting appetizer or side dish.

These Himmel und Erde bites are a flavorful and satisfying dish that celebrates the simple but delicious combination of apples and potatoes. Enjoy them as a taste of German comfort food!

Brathering (Marinated Fried Herring) on Pumpernickel

Ingredients:

For the marinated herring:

- 4 fresh herring fillets, cleaned and deboned
- 1/2 cup white vinegar
- 1/4 cup water
- 1 onion, thinly sliced
- 1 bay leaf
- 6 whole black peppercorns
- 4 whole allspice berries
- 1 tablespoon sugar
- Salt to taste
- Vegetable oil for frying

For serving:

- Pumpernickel bread, sliced
- Chopped fresh parsley for garnish (optional)
- Lemon wedges (optional)

Instructions:

1. In a shallow dish, combine the white vinegar, water, thinly sliced onion, bay leaf, black peppercorns, allspice berries, sugar, and salt. Stir to dissolve the sugar and salt.
2. Place the herring fillets in the marinade, making sure they are submerged. Cover the dish and refrigerate for at least 4 hours or overnight, allowing the herring to marinate and absorb the flavors.
3. After marinating, remove the herring fillets from the marinade and pat them dry with paper towels.
4. Heat vegetable oil in a large skillet over medium-high heat. Once the oil is hot, add the herring fillets to the skillet, skin-side down. Fry until golden brown and

crispy on both sides, about 3-4 minutes per side. Transfer the fried herring to a plate lined with paper towels to drain excess oil.
5. To serve, place a slice of pumpernickel bread on a serving plate. Top each slice with a fried herring fillet.
6. Garnish the Brathering with chopped fresh parsley and serve with lemon wedges on the side, if desired.
7. Enjoy the Brathering on pumpernickel as a flavorful appetizer or snack, celebrating the rich taste of marinated fried herring with the hearty texture of dark bread.

This dish is perfect for sharing with family and friends, especially during gatherings or celebrations!

Stuffed Mushrooms with Bratwurst and Cheese

Ingredients:

- 16 large mushrooms, cleaned and stems removed
- 1/2 lb bratwurst sausage, casing removed
- 1 small onion, finely chopped
- 2 cloves garlic, minced
- 1/2 cup breadcrumbs
- 1/2 cup shredded cheese (such as cheddar or Gruyère)
- 2 tablespoons chopped fresh parsley
- Salt and pepper to taste
- Olive oil for brushing

Instructions:

1. Preheat your oven to 375°F (190°C). Line a baking sheet with parchment paper or lightly grease it with olive oil.
2. In a skillet, cook the bratwurst sausage over medium heat, breaking it up with a spoon, until browned and cooked through. Remove the sausage from the skillet and set aside.
3. In the same skillet, add a little olive oil if needed, then add the chopped onion and minced garlic. Cook until softened and translucent, about 3-4 minutes.
4. Return the cooked bratwurst sausage to the skillet with the onion and garlic. Stir in the breadcrumbs and cook for an additional 2-3 minutes, allowing the breadcrumbs to absorb the flavors.
5. Remove the skillet from the heat and stir in the shredded cheese and chopped fresh parsley. Season with salt and pepper to taste.
6. Fill each mushroom cap with the bratwurst and cheese mixture, pressing down gently to compact the filling.
7. Place the stuffed mushrooms on the prepared baking sheet. Brush the tops of the mushrooms with olive oil.
8. Bake in the preheated oven for 15-20 minutes, or until the mushrooms are tender and the filling is golden brown and bubbly.
9. Remove the stuffed mushrooms from the oven and let them cool slightly before serving.

10. Serve the stuffed mushrooms with bratwurst and cheese hot as a delicious appetizer or snack.

These stuffed mushrooms are sure to be a hit with your family and friends. Enjoy the savory combination of bratwurst and cheese stuffed into tender mushroom caps!

Baked Camembert with Cranberry Sauce and Pretzel Crisps

Ingredients:

- 1 whole Camembert cheese
- 1/4 cup cranberry sauce (homemade or store-bought)
- Pretzel crisps or breadsticks for serving

Instructions:

1. Preheat your oven to 350°F (175°C).
2. Remove any packaging from the Camembert cheese and place it in a small oven-safe baking dish or on a baking sheet lined with parchment paper.
3. Use a sharp knife to score a shallow crosshatch pattern on the top of the Camembert cheese.
4. Spoon the cranberry sauce over the top of the Camembert cheese, spreading it evenly to cover the surface.
5. Bake the Camembert cheese in the preheated oven for 10-15 minutes, or until the cheese is soft and gooey and the cranberry sauce is bubbling.
6. Remove the baked Camembert cheese from the oven and let it cool slightly for a few minutes.
7. Serve the baked Camembert cheese with cranberry sauce alongside pretzel crisps or breadsticks for dipping.
8. Enjoy the creamy, gooey goodness of the baked Camembert cheese paired with the tartness of the cranberry sauce and the crunch of the pretzel crisps.

This appetizer is perfect for holiday gatherings, parties, or any occasion where you want to impress your guests with a delicious and easy-to-make dish!

Matjes Herring Canapés with Pickles and Red Onion

Ingredients:

- Matjes herring fillets (pickled herring)
- Cocktail rye bread or baguette slices, thinly sliced
- Cream cheese or crème fraîche
- Pickles, thinly sliced
- Red onion, thinly sliced
- Fresh dill, chopped (for garnish)
- Lemon wedges (optional)

Instructions:

1. If the Matjes herring fillets are large, cut them into smaller pieces that will fit nicely on your canapés.
2. Toast or lightly grill the slices of cocktail rye bread or baguette until they are crispy and golden brown.
3. Spread a thin layer of cream cheese or crème fraîche on each slice of toasted bread.
4. Place a piece of Matjes herring fillet on top of the cream cheese or crème fraîche layer.
5. Top each herring fillet with a slice of pickle and a few thin slices of red onion.
6. Garnish the canapés with chopped fresh dill.
7. Optionally, serve the Matjes herring canapés with lemon wedges on the side for squeezing over the top.
8. Arrange the canapés on a serving platter and serve immediately.

These Matjes herring canapés are a perfect appetizer for parties, gatherings, or any occasion where you want to impress your guests with a taste of traditional German cuisine. Enjoy the combination of flavors and textures in each bite!

Käsewürfel (German Cheese Cubes) with Grapes

Ingredients:

- Assorted cheeses (such as cheddar, Gouda, Swiss, or Brie), cut into cubes
- Red and green grapes, washed and dried
- Toothpicks or cocktail skewers

Instructions:

1. Cut the assorted cheeses into bite-sized cubes, about 1 inch in size.
2. Wash and dry the red and green grapes, leaving them whole.
3. Thread one cheese cube onto each toothpick or cocktail skewer, followed by one grape.
4. Repeat the process until you've filled all the toothpicks or skewers, alternating between cheese cubes and grapes.
5. Arrange the Käsewürfel skewers on a serving platter.
6. Serve the Käsewürfel skewers with grapes as a tasty and elegant appetizer or snack.

These Käsewürfel skewers with grapes are perfect for parties, gatherings, or any occasion where you want to offer a simple and satisfying snack with a touch of elegance. Enjoy the combination of creamy cheese and juicy grapes in each bite!

Weisswurst Bites with Sweet Mustard and Pretzel Sticks

Ingredients:

- Weisswurst (Bavarian white sausage), cooked and sliced into bite-sized pieces
- Sweet mustard (such as Bavarian or Dijon mustard)
- Pretzel sticks or pretzel rods

Instructions:

1. Cook the Weisswurst according to package instructions. Once cooked, slice the Weisswurst into bite-sized pieces.
2. Serve the Weisswurst bites with sweet mustard for dipping. You can either serve the mustard in a bowl alongside the Weisswurst or drizzle it over the sausage bites.
3. Arrange pretzel sticks or pretzel rods on a serving platter or in a tall glass.
4. Serve the Weisswurst bites with sweet mustard alongside the pretzel sticks.
5. Optionally, garnish the platter with fresh herbs or Bavarian-style garnishes such as radishes or pickles for added flavor and presentation.

Enjoy these Weisswurst bites with sweet mustard and pretzel sticks as a delicious appetizer or snack, perfect for Oktoberfest celebrations or any time you're craving a taste of Bavarian cuisine!

Rouladen Skewers with Mustard and Pickles

Ingredients:

- Thinly sliced beef (such as flank steak or top round), cut into strips
- Dijon mustard
- Pickles, sliced into thin strips
- Wooden skewers or toothpicks

Instructions:

1. Preheat your grill or grill pan over medium-high heat.
2. Lay out the strips of beef on a clean work surface. Spread a thin layer of Dijon mustard on each strip of beef.
3. Place a strip of pickle along one edge of each strip of beef.
4. Roll up each strip of beef with the pickle inside, creating a small, tight roll.
5. Thread the rolled-up beef onto wooden skewers or secure them with toothpicks to keep them from unraveling.
6. Repeat the process until all the beef strips are rolled and skewered.
7. Grill the Rouladen skewers for 2-3 minutes per side, or until the beef is cooked to your desired level of doneness and has nice grill marks.
8. Remove the skewers from the grill and let them rest for a few minutes before serving.
9. Serve the Rouladen skewers with mustard for dipping and extra pickles on the side, if desired.
10. Enjoy these flavorful Rouladen skewers with mustard and pickles as a delicious appetizer or main dish!

These Rouladen skewers offer all the savory goodness of the traditional German dish in a convenient and easy-to-eat format, making them perfect for parties, gatherings, or weeknight dinners.

Labskaus Crostini (North German Corned Beef Hash) on Baguette Slices

Ingredients:

- 1 can (12 oz) corned beef
- 2 large potatoes, boiled and mashed
- 1 small onion, finely chopped
- 2 tablespoons butter
- Salt and pepper to taste
- Baguette, sliced into rounds
- Olive oil for drizzling
- Optional garnishes: chopped fresh parsley, capers, pickles

Instructions:

1. Preheat your oven to 375°F (190°C).
2. In a skillet, melt the butter over medium heat. Add the chopped onion and cook until soft and translucent, about 5 minutes.
3. Add the corned beef to the skillet and break it up with a spoon. Cook, stirring occasionally, until heated through and slightly browned, about 5-7 minutes.
4. Stir in the mashed potatoes, mixing well to combine. Cook for another 2-3 minutes until the flavors meld together. Season with salt and pepper to taste.
5. While the Labskaus mixture is cooking, arrange the baguette slices on a baking sheet. Drizzle olive oil over the slices.
6. Toast the baguette slices in the preheated oven for about 5-7 minutes, or until they are golden brown and crispy.
7. Remove the baguette slices from the oven and let them cool slightly.
8. Spoon a small amount of the Labskaus mixture onto each baguette slice, spreading it evenly.
9. If desired, garnish each crostini with chopped fresh parsley, capers, or pickles.
10. Serve the Labskaus crostini immediately as an appetizer or snack.

These Labskaus crostini are a delicious and creative way to enjoy the flavors of North German cuisine. They're perfect for parties, gatherings, or simply as a unique and tasty snack!

Obatzda-Stuffed Mini Bell Peppers

Ingredients:

- 12 mini bell peppers, halved and seeds removed
- 8 oz Camembert cheese, at room temperature
- 4 oz cream cheese, at room temperature
- 2 tablespoons butter, softened
- 1 small onion, finely chopped
- 1 clove garlic, minced
- 1 tablespoon sweet paprika
- 1 tablespoon caraway seeds
- Salt and pepper to taste
- Chopped fresh chives for garnish (optional)

Instructions:

1. Preheat your oven to 375°F (190°C).
2. In a mixing bowl, combine the Camembert cheese, cream cheese, and butter. Mix until smooth and well combined.
3. Add the chopped onion, minced garlic, sweet paprika, and caraway seeds to the cheese mixture. Season with salt and pepper to taste. Mix until all ingredients are evenly incorporated.
4. Stuff each mini bell pepper half with the Obatzda cheese mixture, filling them generously.
5. Place the stuffed mini bell peppers on a baking sheet lined with parchment paper.
6. Bake in the preheated oven for 12-15 minutes, or until the peppers are tender and the cheese is melted and bubbly.
7. Remove the stuffed mini bell peppers from the oven and let them cool slightly.
8. Garnish the Obatzda-stuffed mini bell peppers with chopped fresh chives, if desired.
9. Serve the stuffed peppers warm as a delicious appetizer or snack.

These Obatzda-stuffed mini bell peppers are sure to be a hit at your next gathering or party. Enjoy the creamy, flavorful filling paired with the sweetness of the peppers!

Liptauer Cheese Spread with Radishes and Rye Bread

Ingredients:

For the Liptauer cheese spread:

- 8 oz cream cheese, softened
- 1/4 cup unsalted butter, softened
- 2 tablespoons sweet paprika
- 2 tablespoons Dijon mustard
- 2 tablespoons capers, drained and chopped
- 2 tablespoons finely chopped red onion
- 1 tablespoon caraway seeds
- 1 tablespoon Worcestershire sauce
- 1 teaspoon anchovy paste (optional)
- Salt and pepper to taste

For serving:

- Radishes, thinly sliced
- Rye bread, sliced

Instructions:

1. In a mixing bowl, combine the softened cream cheese and unsalted butter. Mix until smooth and well combined.
2. Add the sweet paprika, Dijon mustard, chopped capers, finely chopped red onion, caraway seeds, Worcestershire sauce, and anchovy paste (if using) to the cream cheese mixture. Mix until all ingredients are evenly incorporated.
3. Season the Liptauer cheese spread with salt and pepper to taste. Adjust the seasoning according to your preference.
4. Transfer the Liptauer cheese spread to a serving bowl and refrigerate for at least 1 hour to allow the flavors to meld together.
5. Before serving, arrange the thinly sliced radishes and sliced rye bread on a serving platter.

6. Serve the Liptauer cheese spread alongside the radishes and rye bread.
7. Optionally, garnish the Liptauer cheese spread with additional chopped herbs such as parsley or chives for a pop of color and flavor.
8. Enjoy the Liptauer cheese spread with radishes and rye bread as a delicious appetizer or snack.

This flavorful spread pairs perfectly with the crunchy texture of radishes and the earthy taste of rye bread, making it a delightful addition to any gathering or party!

Black Forest Ham and Cheese Pinwheels

Ingredients:

- 1 sheet puff pastry, thawed
- 6 slices Black Forest ham
- 6 slices Swiss cheese
- 2 tablespoons Dijon mustard
- 1 egg, beaten (for egg wash)
- Sesame seeds or poppy seeds (optional, for garnish)

Instructions:

1. Preheat your oven to 400°F (200°C). Line a baking sheet with parchment paper.
2. On a lightly floured surface, roll out the puff pastry sheet into a rectangle, about 10x12 inches.
3. Spread the Dijon mustard evenly over the puff pastry sheet, leaving a small border around the edges.
4. Layer the Black Forest ham slices evenly over the mustard-covered puff pastry sheet.
5. Place the Swiss cheese slices on top of the ham, covering the entire surface.
6. Starting from one of the long edges, tightly roll up the puff pastry sheet into a log.
7. Using a sharp knife, slice the log into 1-inch thick pinwheels.
8. Place the pinwheels on the prepared baking sheet, leaving some space between each pinwheel.
9. Brush the tops of the pinwheels with the beaten egg. This will give them a golden brown color when baked.
10. If desired, sprinkle sesame seeds or poppy seeds over the tops of the pinwheels for added texture and flavor.
11. Bake in the preheated oven for 15-20 minutes, or until the pinwheels are puffed and golden brown.
12. Remove from the oven and let cool slightly before serving.
13. Serve the Black Forest ham and cheese pinwheels warm as a delicious appetizer or snack.

These pinwheels are perfect for parties, gatherings, or as a tasty treat for any occasion. Enjoy the combination of savory Black Forest ham and Swiss cheese wrapped in flaky puff pastry!

Knackwurst Coins with Spicy Mustard Sauce

Ingredients:

- 1 lb Knackwurst sausages, sliced into coins
- 1/2 cup spicy mustard (such as Dijon or whole grain mustard)
- 2 tablespoons honey
- 1 tablespoon apple cider vinegar
- 1 clove garlic, minced
- Salt and pepper to taste
- Chopped fresh parsley for garnish (optional)

Instructions:

1. In a small bowl, whisk together the spicy mustard, honey, apple cider vinegar, minced garlic, salt, and pepper to make the spicy mustard sauce. Adjust the seasoning to taste.
2. Heat a skillet or frying pan over medium heat. Add the Knackwurst coins to the skillet and cook until they are browned and heated through, about 5-7 minutes, stirring occasionally.
3. Once the Knackwurst coins are cooked, transfer them to a serving platter.
4. Drizzle the spicy mustard sauce over the cooked Knackwurst coins or serve it on the side as a dipping sauce.
5. Garnish the Knackwurst coins with chopped fresh parsley, if desired, for added color and flavor.
6. Serve the Knackwurst coins with spicy mustard sauce immediately as a delicious appetizer or snack.

These Knackwurst coins with spicy mustard sauce are sure to be a hit at your next gathering or party. Enjoy the savory flavor of the Knackwurst paired with the tangy and spicy mustard sauce!

Bavarian Ham and Cheese Spread on Pumpernickel Rounds

Ingredients:

- 1/2 lb Bavarian ham, finely chopped
- 4 oz cream cheese, softened
- 1/4 cup sour cream
- 1/4 cup mayonnaise
- 1 tablespoon Dijon mustard
- 1 tablespoon honey
- 1 cup shredded Swiss cheese
- Salt and pepper to taste
- Pumpernickel rounds or slices
- Fresh parsley or chives for garnish (optional)

Instructions:

1. In a mixing bowl, combine the finely chopped Bavarian ham, softened cream cheese, sour cream, mayonnaise, Dijon mustard, and honey. Mix until smooth and well combined.
2. Stir in the shredded Swiss cheese until evenly distributed throughout the mixture.
3. Season the ham and cheese spread with salt and pepper to taste. Adjust the seasoning according to your preference.
4. Arrange the pumpernickel rounds or slices on a serving platter.
5. Spread a generous amount of the ham and cheese mixture onto each pumpernickel round.
6. If desired, garnish each pumpernickel round with chopped fresh parsley or chives for added flavor and presentation.
7. Serve the Bavarian ham and cheese spread on pumpernickel rounds immediately as a delicious appetizer or snack.

These savory and creamy bites are perfect for parties, gatherings, or any occasion where you want to impress your guests with a taste of Bavarian cuisine. Enjoy the rich flavor of the ham and cheese spread paired with the hearty texture of pumpernickel!

German Meat and Cheese Platter with Mustard and Pickles

Ingredients:

For the meat and cheese selection:

- Assorted German meats such as Black Forest ham, Bavarian salami, and smoked sausage
- Assorted German cheeses such as Emmental, Gouda, and Limburger
- Pickles, such as gherkins or cornichons
- Mustard, such as Dijon or whole grain
- Dark bread or pretzels, for serving

Instructions:

1. Start by selecting a variety of German meats and cheeses. Arrange them on a large platter or wooden board, leaving space in between each item.
2. Place small bowls or ramekins of mustard on the platter, spacing them out among the meats and cheeses.
3. Add a handful of pickles to the platter, arranging them around the meats and cheeses.
4. If desired, garnish the platter with fresh herbs or sliced fruits, such as grapes or apples, for added color and flavor.
5. Serve the German meat and cheese platter with mustard and pickles alongside dark bread or pretzels for an authentic and delicious snack or appetizer.

This platter is perfect for sharing with friends and family at parties, gatherings, or as a tasty addition to a charcuterie board. Enjoy the rich flavors and variety of German meats and cheeses paired with tangy mustard and crunchy pickles!

Krabbenbrot (North Sea Shrimp Sandwiches) on Rye Bread

Ingredients:

- Rye bread slices or rolls
- North Sea shrimp (also known as brown shrimp or crangon crangon)
- Butter or mayonnaise
- Lemon juice
- Salt and pepper to taste
- Optional garnishes: sliced cucumber, lettuce, radishes, dill, chives

Instructions:

1. Start by preparing your rye bread slices or rolls. You can lightly toast them if desired.
2. If using butter, spread a thin layer on each slice of rye bread. Alternatively, you can use mayonnaise as a spread.
3. Rinse the North Sea shrimp under cold water and pat them dry with a paper towel. Place the shrimp in a bowl.
4. Squeeze a little lemon juice over the shrimp and season with salt and pepper to taste. Toss gently to coat the shrimp evenly.
5. Arrange the seasoned North Sea shrimp on top of the buttered or mayonnaise-spread rye bread slices.
6. If desired, add optional garnishes such as sliced cucumber, lettuce, radishes, dill, or chives on top of the shrimp.
7. Close the sandwiches with another slice of rye bread or serve open-faced.
8. Serve the Krabbenbrot (North Sea shrimp sandwiches) immediately as a delicious snack or light meal.

These sandwiches are perfect for a quick lunch, a light dinner, or as part of a brunch spread. Enjoy the fresh flavors of the North Sea shrimp paired with the hearty taste of rye bread!

Currywurst Potato Skins with Curry Ketchup

Ingredients:

- 4 large russet potatoes
- Olive oil
- Salt and pepper to taste
- 1 cup curry ketchup (store-bought or homemade)
- 1 tablespoon curry powder
- 1 tablespoon honey or brown sugar
- Cooked bratwurst or sausage, sliced into coins
- Chopped fresh parsley for garnish (optional)

Instructions:

1. Preheat your oven to 400°F (200°C).
2. Scrub the potatoes clean and pat them dry. Pierce each potato several times with a fork.
3. Rub the potatoes with olive oil and sprinkle them with salt and pepper.
4. Place the potatoes directly on the oven rack and bake for 45-60 minutes, or until they are tender when pierced with a fork.
5. While the potatoes are baking, prepare the curry ketchup. In a small saucepan, combine the curry ketchup, curry powder, and honey or brown sugar. Heat over medium-low heat, stirring occasionally, until warmed through and the flavors are well combined.
6. Once the potatoes are baked and cool enough to handle, cut them in half lengthwise. Scoop out the flesh, leaving about 1/4 inch of potato attached to the skins. Save the potato flesh for another use, such as mashed potatoes.
7. Brush the inside and outside of the potato skins with olive oil. Place them back on the baking sheet, cut side up.
8. Fill each potato skin with a spoonful of curry ketchup, then top with sliced bratwurst or sausage coins.
9. Return the filled potato skins to the oven and bake for an additional 10-15 minutes, or until the toppings are heated through and the skins are crispy.
10. Remove the currywurst potato skins from the oven and let them cool slightly.
11. Garnish the potato skins with chopped fresh parsley, if desired.

12. Serve the currywurst potato skins with extra curry ketchup on the side for dipping.

These currywurst potato skins are perfect for parties, game day snacks, or anytime you're craving a delicious and unique appetizer inspired by German street food!

Gruyère and Leek Tartlets

Ingredients:

- 1 sheet of puff pastry, thawed
- 1 tablespoon butter
- 2 leeks, white and light green parts only, thinly sliced
- Salt and pepper to taste
- 1 cup Gruyère cheese, shredded
- 1/4 cup heavy cream
- 2 eggs
- Fresh thyme leaves for garnish (optional)

Instructions:

1. Preheat your oven to 375°F (190°C). Lightly grease a muffin tin or tartlet pan.
2. Roll out the puff pastry on a lightly floured surface and cut out circles slightly larger than the muffin tin cavities or tartlet pan wells.
3. Press the puff pastry circles into the muffin tin cavities or tartlet pan wells, forming little tartlet shells. Prick the bottoms of the pastry shells with a fork.
4. In a skillet, melt the butter over medium heat. Add the sliced leeks and sauté until they are softened, about 5-7 minutes. Season with salt and pepper to taste.
5. Divide the sautéed leeks evenly among the puff pastry shells.
6. Sprinkle the shredded Gruyère cheese over the leeks in each pastry shell.
7. In a small bowl, whisk together the heavy cream and eggs until well combined. Season with a pinch of salt and pepper.
8. Carefully pour the egg mixture into each pastry shell, filling them almost to the top.
9. Bake the tartlets in the preheated oven for 15-20 minutes, or until the pastry is golden brown and the filling is set.
10. Remove the tartlets from the oven and let them cool slightly in the pan.
11. Once cooled, carefully remove the tartlets from the muffin tin or tartlet pan and transfer them to a serving platter.
12. Garnish the Gruyère and leek tartlets with fresh thyme leaves, if desired.

These Gruyère and leek tartlets are best served warm or at room temperature. They make a delicious appetizer for parties, brunches, or any special occasion!

Kartoffelbrötchen (German Potato Rolls) with Butter and Sea Salt

Ingredients:

- 1 cup mashed potatoes (made from boiled potatoes, cooled)
- 2 1/4 teaspoons (1 packet) active dry yeast
- 1/4 cup warm water (110°F/45°C)
- 1 tablespoon granulated sugar
- 3 1/2 cups all-purpose flour
- 1 teaspoon salt
- 1/4 cup unsalted butter, melted
- Butter for serving
- Coarse sea salt for sprinkling

Instructions:

1. In a small bowl, combine the warm water and sugar. Sprinkle the yeast over the water and let it sit for about 5-10 minutes, or until foamy.
2. In a large mixing bowl, combine the mashed potatoes, flour, and salt. Mix well.
3. Add the activated yeast mixture and melted butter to the flour mixture. Stir until a dough forms.
4. Turn the dough out onto a floured surface and knead for about 5-7 minutes, or until the dough is smooth and elastic.
5. Place the dough in a greased bowl, cover with a clean kitchen towel or plastic wrap, and let it rise in a warm, draft-free place for about 1-1.5 hours, or until doubled in size.
6. Once the dough has risen, punch it down and divide it into 12 equal portions. Shape each portion into a round roll and place them on a parchment-lined baking sheet, spaced a few inches apart.
7. Cover the rolls with a clean kitchen towel and let them rise again for about 30-45 minutes, or until puffy.
8. Preheat your oven to 375°F (190°C).
9. Bake the rolls in the preheated oven for 15-20 minutes, or until they are golden brown on top and sound hollow when tapped on the bottom.
10. Remove the rolls from the oven and let them cool on a wire rack for a few minutes.
11. Serve the Kartoffelbrötchen warm with butter and a sprinkle of coarse sea salt.

These German potato rolls are best enjoyed fresh from the oven, but you can also store them in an airtight container once cooled and reheat them before serving. They're perfect for breakfast, brunch, or as a side for soups and stews!

Obatzda-Stuffed Pretzel Bites

Ingredients:

For the Obatzda filling:

- 8 oz Camembert cheese, at room temperature
- 4 oz cream cheese, at room temperature
- 2 tablespoons unsalted butter, softened
- 1/4 cup finely chopped red onion
- 2 tablespoons chopped chives
- 1 tablespoon sweet paprika
- 1 tablespoon caraway seeds
- Salt and pepper to taste

For the pretzel dough:

- 1 1/2 cups warm water (110°F/45°C)
- 1 tablespoon granulated sugar
- 2 teaspoons active dry yeast
- 4 cups all-purpose flour
- 1 teaspoon salt
- 1/4 cup baking soda
- 1 egg, beaten, for egg wash
- Coarse sea salt for sprinkling

Instructions:

1. Start by making the Obatzda filling. In a mixing bowl, combine the Camembert cheese, cream cheese, and softened butter. Mix until smooth and well combined.
2. Add the finely chopped red onion, chopped chives, sweet paprika, caraway seeds, salt, and pepper to the cheese mixture. Mix until all ingredients are evenly incorporated. Taste and adjust seasoning if needed. Refrigerate the Obatzda filling while you prepare the pretzel dough.
3. In a small bowl, combine the warm water, sugar, and active dry yeast. Let it sit for about 5-10 minutes, or until foamy.

4. In a large mixing bowl, combine the flour and salt. Pour the yeast mixture into the flour mixture and stir until a dough forms.
5. Turn the dough out onto a floured surface and knead for about 5-7 minutes, or until the dough is smooth and elastic. Add more flour if the dough is too sticky.
6. Divide the dough into smaller portions and roll each portion into a ball.
7. Flatten each dough ball into a small circle. Place a small spoonful of the Obatzda filling in the center of each circle.
8. Fold the edges of the dough up and around the filling, pinching the seams tightly to seal.
9. Preheat your oven to 425°F (220°C). Line a baking sheet with parchment paper.
10. In a large pot, bring water to a boil. Once boiling, add the baking soda and reduce the heat to medium-low.
11. Carefully drop the stuffed pretzel bites into the boiling water, a few at a time, and cook for about 30 seconds. Remove them with a slotted spoon and place them on the prepared baking sheet.
12. Brush the tops of the pretzel bites with beaten egg wash and sprinkle them with coarse sea salt.
13. Bake in the preheated oven for 12-15 minutes, or until the pretzel bites are golden brown and cooked through.
14. Remove from the oven and let cool slightly before serving.
15. Serve the Obatzda-stuffed pretzel bites warm as a delicious appetizer or snack.

These Obatzda-stuffed pretzel bites are sure to be a hit at your next gathering or party, combining the flavors of Bavaria in a delightful bite-sized form!

German Ham and Cheese Sliders with Poppy Seed Glaze

Ingredients:

For the sliders:

- 12 slider rolls or dinner rolls
- 1/2 lb Black Forest ham, thinly sliced
- 6 slices Swiss cheese
- 1/4 cup unsalted butter, melted
- 1 tablespoon Dijon mustard
- 1 tablespoon Worcestershire sauce
- 1 tablespoon poppy seeds
- 1 teaspoon onion powder
- 1/2 teaspoon garlic powder

Instructions:

1. Preheat your oven to 350°F (175°C). Lightly grease a baking dish or line it with parchment paper.
2. Without separating the rolls, slice the slider rolls in half horizontally and place the bottom half in the prepared baking dish.
3. Layer the Black Forest ham evenly over the bottom half of the rolls, followed by the Swiss cheese slices.
4. Place the top half of the rolls over the cheese to close the sliders.
5. In a small bowl, whisk together the melted butter, Dijon mustard, Worcestershire sauce, poppy seeds, onion powder, and garlic powder until well combined.
6. Pour the butter mixture evenly over the tops of the sliders, making sure to coat each roll.
7. Cover the baking dish with aluminum foil and bake in the preheated oven for 15-20 minutes, or until the cheese is melted and the sliders are heated through.
8. Remove the foil and bake for an additional 5 minutes, or until the tops are golden brown and slightly crispy.
9. Remove the sliders from the oven and let them cool slightly before serving.
10. Serve the German ham and cheese sliders with poppy seed glaze warm as a delicious appetizer or snack.

These sliders are perfect for parties, game day gatherings, or any occasion where you want to impress your guests with a tasty and satisfying dish!

Sauerkraut and Cheese Stuffed Mushrooms

Ingredients:

- 16 large mushrooms, cleaned with stems removed
- 1 cup sauerkraut, drained and squeezed dry
- 1 cup shredded Swiss cheese
- 1/4 cup grated Parmesan cheese
- 2 cloves garlic, minced
- 2 tablespoons olive oil
- 2 tablespoons chopped fresh parsley
- Salt and pepper to taste

Instructions:

1. Preheat your oven to 375°F (190°C). Line a baking sheet with parchment paper.
2. In a skillet, heat the olive oil over medium heat. Add the minced garlic and sauté for 1-2 minutes, until fragrant.
3. Add the sauerkraut to the skillet and cook for another 3-4 minutes, stirring occasionally, until heated through and any excess moisture has evaporated.
4. Remove the skillet from the heat and let the sauerkraut mixture cool slightly.
5. In a mixing bowl, combine the sauerkraut mixture, shredded Swiss cheese, grated Parmesan cheese, chopped parsley, salt, and pepper. Mix well to combine.
6. Stuff each mushroom cap with the sauerkraut and cheese mixture, pressing it down gently to fill the cavity.
7. Place the stuffed mushrooms on the prepared baking sheet.
8. Bake in the preheated oven for 15-20 minutes, or until the mushrooms are tender and the filling is golden and bubbly.
9. Remove the stuffed mushrooms from the oven and let them cool slightly before serving.
10. Serve the sauerkraut and cheese stuffed mushrooms warm as a delicious appetizer or side dish.

These stuffed mushrooms are perfect for parties, gatherings, or as a flavorful addition to your holiday table. Enjoy the tangy sauerkraut paired with the creamy Swiss cheese in every bite!

Sardinenbrot (German Sardine Sandwiches) on Rye Bread

Ingredients:

- Rye bread slices
- Canned sardines in oil or water, drained
- Butter or mayonnaise
- Red onion, thinly sliced
- Lemon wedges, for serving
- Optional garnishes: lettuce leaves, cucumber slices, radish slices, capers, fresh herbs (such as parsley or dill)

Instructions:

1. Begin by lightly toasting the rye bread slices, if desired.
2. Spread a thin layer of butter or mayonnaise on each slice of rye bread.
3. Arrange the drained sardines on top of the buttered or mayonnaise-spread rye bread slices.
4. Top the sardines with thinly sliced red onion.
5. If desired, add optional garnishes such as lettuce leaves, cucumber slices, radish slices, capers, or fresh herbs.
6. Serve the Sardinenbrot sandwiches with lemon wedges on the side for squeezing over the sardines.
7. Enjoy the sandwiches immediately as a delicious and satisfying meal or snack.

These German Sardinenbrot sandwiches are simple to make and packed with flavor and nutrients from the sardines and other toppings. They're perfect for a quick lunch at home or to take with you on the go!

Würstchen im Schlafrock (Sausages in Blankets) with Mustard Dip

Ingredients:

For the sausages in blankets:

- 12 cocktail sausages or Frankfurter sausages
- 1 sheet puff pastry, thawed
- Flour, for dusting
- 1 egg, beaten (for egg wash)
- Sesame seeds or poppy seeds (optional, for garnish)

For the mustard dip:

- 1/4 cup mayonnaise
- 2 tablespoons Dijon mustard
- 1 tablespoon honey
- 1 tablespoon lemon juice
- Salt and pepper to taste

Instructions:

1. Preheat your oven to 400°F (200°C). Line a baking sheet with parchment paper.
2. Roll out the puff pastry on a lightly floured surface. Cut it into thin strips wide enough to wrap around each sausage.
3. Wrap each cocktail sausage or Frankfurter sausage with a strip of puff pastry, leaving the ends slightly exposed.
4. Place the wrapped sausages on the prepared baking sheet.
5. Brush the tops of the puff pastry-wrapped sausages with beaten egg wash. If desired, sprinkle sesame seeds or poppy seeds on top for garnish.
6. Bake in the preheated oven for 15-20 minutes, or until the puff pastry is golden brown and puffed up.
7. While the sausages in blankets are baking, prepare the mustard dip. In a small bowl, whisk together the mayonnaise, Dijon mustard, honey, lemon juice, salt, and pepper until smooth and well combined. Adjust the seasoning to taste.

8. Once the sausages in blankets are done baking, remove them from the oven and let them cool slightly.
9. Serve the sausages in blankets warm with the mustard dip on the side for dipping.

These Würstchen im Schlafrock are best enjoyed fresh from the oven, while the puff pastry is still warm and flaky. They make a delicious appetizer or snack for parties, game days, or any occasion!

Pfälzer Saumagen (Palatinate Pork Stomach) Bites with Sauerkraut and Mustard

Ingredients:

For the Pfälzer Saumagen bites:

- 1 lb pork belly, finely diced
- 1 lb pork shoulder, finely diced
- 1 lb potatoes, peeled and grated
- 1 large onion, finely chopped
- 2 cloves garlic, minced
- 1 tablespoon marjoram
- 1 teaspoon ground allspice
- Salt and pepper to taste
- 1 large pork stomach (about 2 lbs), cleaned and soaked in salt water overnight
- Cooking twine

For serving:

- Sauerkraut
- Mustard

Instructions:

1. Preheat your oven to 350°F (175°C).
2. In a large mixing bowl, combine the diced pork belly, diced pork shoulder, grated potatoes, chopped onion, minced garlic, marjoram, ground allspice, salt, and pepper. Mix until well combined.
3. Lay the cleaned pork stomach flat on a work surface. Spoon the pork mixture onto the center of the pork stomach.
4. Roll up the pork stomach tightly, encasing the filling. Use cooking twine to tie the roll securely at both ends and in the middle.
5. Place the rolled pork stomach in a roasting pan. Add water to the pan until it reaches about halfway up the sides of the stomach.
6. Cover the roasting pan with aluminum foil and bake in the preheated oven for 2-3 hours, or until the pork stomach is cooked through and tender.

7. Once cooked, remove the pork stomach from the oven and let it cool slightly. Remove the cooking twine and slice the rolled stomach into bite-sized pieces.
8. To serve, arrange the Pfälzer Saumagen bites on a platter alongside sauerkraut and mustard for dipping.

These Pfälzer Saumagen bites are a hearty and flavorful dish that pairs well with the tanginess of sauerkraut and the sharpness of mustard. Enjoy this traditional German dish at your next gathering or celebration!

www.ingramcontent.com/pod-product-compliance
Lightning Source LLC
LaVergne TN
LVHW062048070526
838201LV00080B/2195